WHALES TO THE RESCUE

HOW WHALES HELP ENGINEER THE PLANET

Written by ADRIENNE MASON

Illustrated by KIM SMITH

Kids Can Press

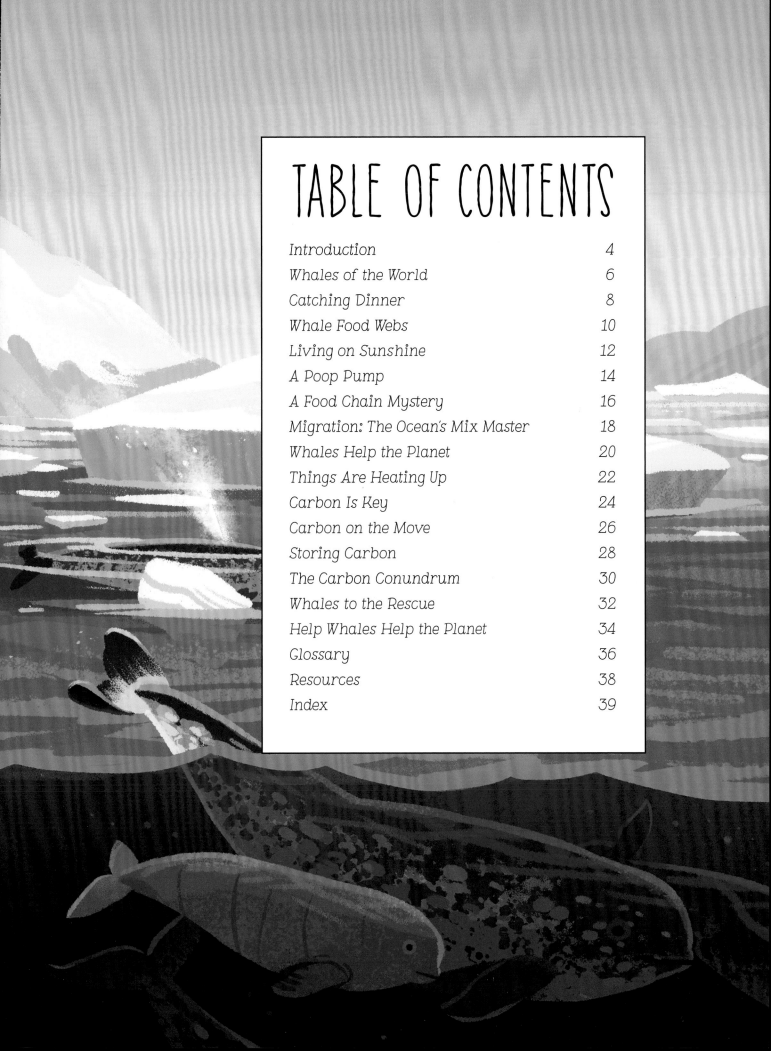

TABLE OF CONTENTS

INTRODUCTION

Off the coast of Trincomalee, Sri Lanka, a sperm whale as long as three minivans dives deep in the ocean, chasing a giant squid. Ten minutes go by, then twenty ... thirty ... forty. Finally, after almost an hour, the whale breaks the ocean's surface with a massive exhale. *Whoosh!* The blast of warm air **condenses** into water droplets that catch the sun's light and glitter briefly before evaporating.

The sperm whale's world may seem foreign — think of all the gear you would need to survive in the ocean. And giant squid for dinner? Maybe not. But sperm whales, and all the world's whales, are actually a lot like you. Just like humans and other mammals, they give birth to live babies that feed on their mother's milk. They're warm-blooded. And while they can hold their breath for long periods as they swim and

dive, they still have to come to the surface to grab gulps of the air we all share.

Whales are found in all the world's oceans, from the Arctic to the Antarctic, from the Atlantic to the Pacific. Since they spend most of their time underwater, whales are still quite mysterious to us. But new research tools are helping us discover many new things about their lives, such as where they travel and how far, what they eat and what might eat them. And one of the most remarkable things we've learned? As whales go about their lives, they're also helping the planet and, ultimately, us!

As they swim and dive and eat and poop, whales are working as **ecosystem engineers**. Their actions help maintain a healthy ocean and can even affect Earth's **atmosphere**, which is critical in a warming world.

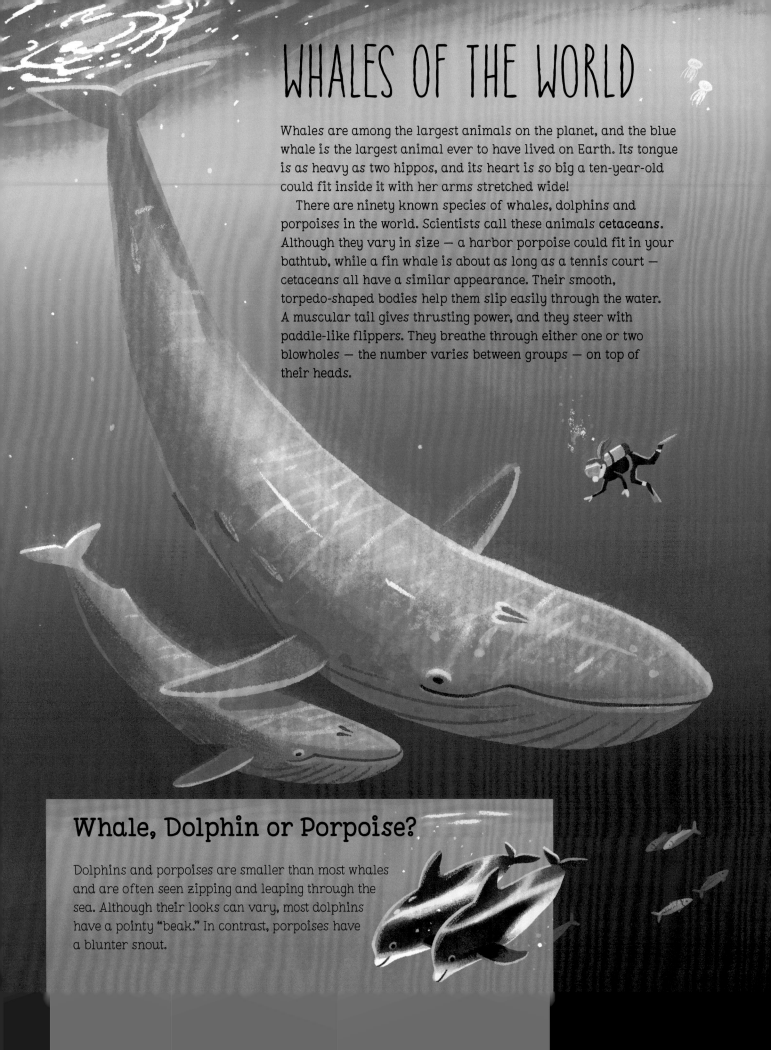

WHALES OF THE WORLD

Whales are among the largest animals on the planet, and the blue whale is the largest animal ever to have lived on Earth. Its tongue is as heavy as two hippos, and its heart is so big a ten-year-old could fit inside it with her arms stretched wide!

There are ninety known species of whales, dolphins and porpoises in the world. Scientists call these animals **cetaceans**. Although they vary in size — a harbor porpoise could fit in your bathtub, while a fin whale is about as long as a tennis court — cetaceans all have a similar appearance. Their smooth, torpedo-shaped bodies help them slip easily through the water. A muscular tail gives thrusting power, and they steer with paddle-like flippers. They breathe through either one or two blowholes — the number varies between groups — on top of their heads.

Whale, Dolphin or Porpoise?

Dolphins and porpoises are smaller than most whales and are often seen zipping and leaping through the sea. Although their looks can vary, most dolphins have a pointy "beak." In contrast, porpoises have a blunter snout.

Know Your Whales

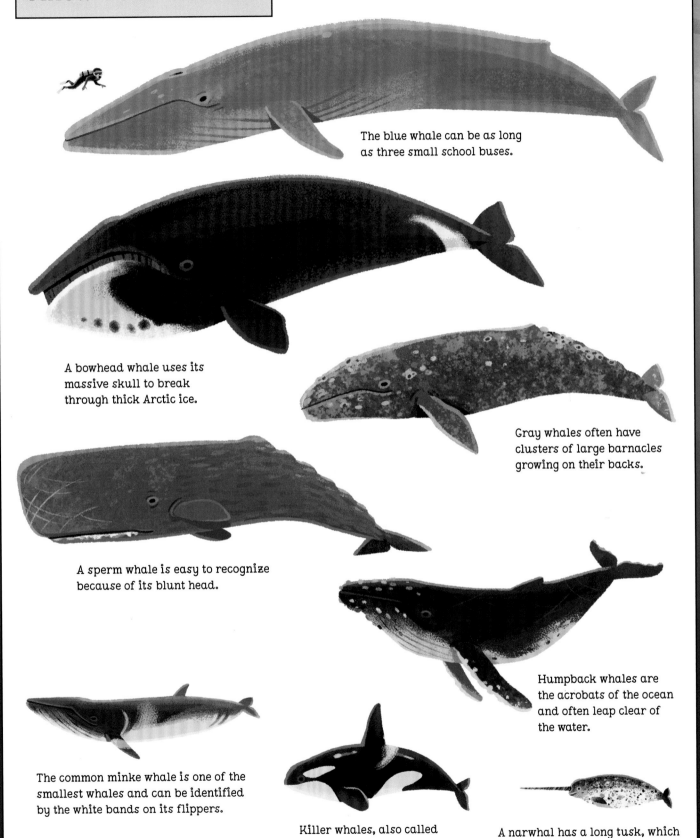

The blue whale can be as long as three small school buses.

A bowhead whale uses its massive skull to break through thick Arctic ice.

Gray whales often have clusters of large barnacles growing on their backs.

A sperm whale is easy to recognize because of its blunt head.

Humpback whales are the acrobats of the ocean and often leap clear of the water.

The common minke whale is one of the smallest whales and can be identified by the white bands on its flippers.

Killer whales, also called orcas, use complex sounds to "talk" with one another.

A narwhal has a long tusk, which is an enlarged spiral tooth.

CATCHING DINNER

Despite being the largest animal on Earth, a blue whale eats some of the smallest animals in the ocean. Most of their diet consists of krill, shrimplike **crustaceans** about as long as two paper clips. But how does such a large animal get such tiny creatures out of the water? It's like you trying to pick grains of rice out of your soup! Blue whales and the other large whales — such as fin, humpback and right whales — are known as **baleen** whales because they use baleen to snare their food.

Baleen is made of **keratin**, the same material as your fingernails. Baleen grows in thin plates that are attached to the whale's upper jaw. They use the baleen to strain their food — krill and other small crustaceans, or even small fish — out of the water.

Baleen whales use various strategies for getting their food. Humpbacks and blue whales open their mouths wide and gulp in seawater. They use their giant tongues to push the water out, snagging any prey in the baleen plates. Bowhead whales swim along the surface with their mouths half open, skimming food. And gray whales often scoop mouthfuls of sand and mud from the seafloor, using their baleen to strain worms and other small animals from the muck.

Other whales, including killer whales, belugas and sperm whales, use their teeth to eat prey such as fish, squid, octopus and sometimes other marine mammals. Some species of toothed whales use sound to find and target their prey. This is called **echolocation**.

Seeing with Sound

To navigate and find food, killer whales, sperm whales and other toothed cetaceans produce rapid pulses and clicks to scan their surroundings. These sounds bounce off objects in their path, and the returning echoes give them information about the seafloor, underwater obstacles and the presence of prey. A sperm whale, for example, sends out a series of clicks, and if the sound hits, say, a squid, the echo bounces back to the whale. Dinner! To home in on the prey, the whale increases the speed of the clicks, which pinpoints its meal.

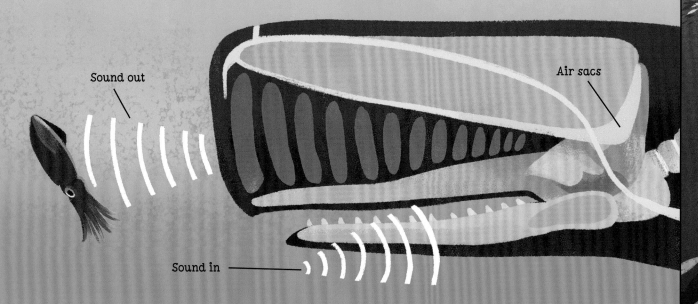

Sound out

Air sacs

Sound in

Sperm whales make the clicks in their nasal passages and air sacs. The sounds come back through their jaw.

WHALE FOOD WEBS

Food is tasty, but the main reason we eat is to get energy. It's the same for all animals. Whether a whale eats krill, fish or even seals, food gives it the energy to stay alive and go about its daily tasks, from hunting to traveling to caring for its young.

In nature, energy flows between living things. We use **food chains** to show these relationships.

The food chains for whales start with **phytoplankton**. These are tiny plantlike **organisms** that convert the energy of the sun into food. They are small and light, so they float near the ocean surface where there is sunlight.

Next in the ocean food chain are **zooplankton**, small animals that float or drift on the ocean currents. They eat phytoplankton or other kinds of zooplankton. Zooplankton includes fully grown animals, such as krill, and the larvae (babies) of animals.

A whale could be part of many different food chains. These chains weave together to make **food webs**, showing all the relationships between living things in an **ecosystem**.

Killer whale

Salmon

Herring

Zooplankton

Humpback whale

Small fish

Phytoplankton

Blue whale

Krill

Sperm whale

Squid

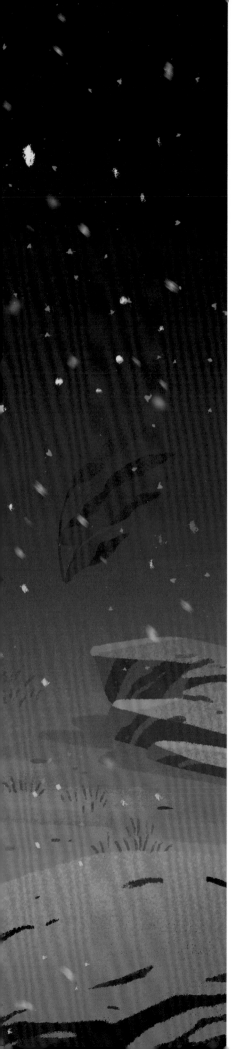

LIVING ON SUNSHINE
(AND POOP AND SKIN, DIRT AND DEAD STUFF)

If you've ever grown a plant, you know that it needs sunlight and food. It's the same for phytoplankton.

Phytoplankton use the chemical **chlorophyll** to capture the energy of the sun in a process called **photosynthesis**. This energy is then passed on to the animals that eat the phytoplankton.

Just as you might add fertilizer to a houseplant to give it a boost, phytoplankton need vitamins, minerals and other nutrients to grow. Nutrients come to the ocean by many different paths:

* Sand and soil ride to the ocean in rivers, and travel on the winds from dust storms and volcanoes.

* As animals grow, they shed parts of their bodies — skin, bits of shell, even the occasional claw or tooth. And, of course, living things eventually die. All the bits of once-living things fall through the water in what scientists call **marine snow**. As they sink, these parts begin to decay, adding nutrients to the seawater. Eventually, they settle on the seafloor to make a nutrient-rich muck.

* Animal waste also provides nutrients. Yup, animals are peeing in the pool! One study found that a fin whale pees 974 L (257 gal.) a day. That's as much liquid as 234 toilet flushes! Then, of course, there's the poop. Whales — and other animals, too — are doing lots of pooping.

All this shedding and dying and peeing and pooping create a nutritious soup in the ocean that feeds the phytoplankton ... which feed the zooplankton ... and so on up the food chain.

Mud Suckers

Among a gray whale's favorite foods are tiny burrowing shrimp and worms, and shrimplike animals called amphipods. Amphipods live on the seafloor where they **scavenge** for food. Gray whales scoop up the mud, the amphipods and the food-rich gunk on the seafloor, then filter it all through their short baleen.

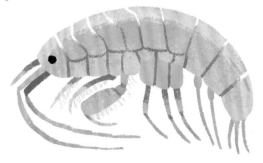

A POOP PUMP

Call it what you like — scat, feces, doo-doo or dung — but all animals make it. Pooping is how animals get rid of undigested food.

The great baleen whales — such as blue, fin and sei whales — are powerful poopers. Every day, they dive deep into the ocean to feed on krill and other types of zooplankton. Upon surfacing, they release big plumes of poop. And when that happens, it's a happy day for the phytoplankton floating near the sea surface. That poop delivers a blast of nutrients they can use to grow and reproduce.

Across the world's oceans, whales are part of a massive poop pump — taking nutrients from the deep and making "special deliveries" to the surface. And since just one large whale eats more than 10 t (10 tn.) of food a day, they're adding a lot of poop to the sea!

As whales dive, they're also mixing and churning the water. Like giant plungers, they help drive nutrients, as well as **algae** and animals, up and down through the water column. Phytoplankton, for instance, need to be near the ocean's surface to capture the energy of the sun. Over time, though, they start to sink and eventually drift beyond the sun's rays. But the powerful thrust of a surfacing whale can punt the phytoplankton back to the surface. Once there, they might just find themselves in an energizing bath of whale fertilizer, helping them to grow and reproduce.

More whales mean more poop. More poop means more phytoplankton. And more phytoplankton drive ocean food chains, fueling everything from fish and squid to crabs and clams.

In the ocean, whale poop makes the world go round!

A FOOD CHAIN MYSTERY

Researchers trying to solve a math mystery helped us learn about the poop pump. They were thinking about the great baleen whales of the Antarctic and their favorite food: krill.

The researchers knew that one hundred or more years ago, there were a lot more whales in the Southern Ocean around Antarctica. (It's estimated that nine out of every ten whales in those regions were killed by whalers.) They also knew that when the ocean was filled with whales, it was filled with krill, too. Those big baleen whales have big appetites. A blue whale can eat up to 16 t (17.6 tn.) a day. One massive gulp of krill can contain close to 500 000 calories — to get that many calories, you'd have to eat more than 83 000 peanuts!

So here was the puzzle: Where did all the krill go? You would think that with the population of hungry whales so reduced, the krill population would increase. Instead, it shrank.

To solve the puzzle, the researchers started to look closely at the whales' food. They found that krill are rich in iron, an **element** they need to grow and reproduce. This was curious, because researchers knew from their studies of ocean chemistry that there wasn't that much iron in the Southern Ocean. They also knew that iron is critical for phytoplankton. When iron is scarce, phytoplankton don't grow as well.

So where were the krill getting their iron? Where was it coming from? The math problem was solved by looking at nutrient cycles and food chains.

Phytoplankton absorb what little iron there is in the ocean.

Krill eat phytoplankton and concentrate the iron even more in their tissues.

Then whales cruise the oceans, gorging on krill, krill and more krill.

When the whales come to the surface, they release a slurry of bright red — and iron-rich — poop.

One study showed that whale poop had *ten million times* more iron in it than the seawater had! The whales' rich fertilizer feeds the phytoplankton, which drive ocean food chains.

Mystery solved. All parts of the food chain — from iron to phytoplankton to krill to whales (and their poop) — were needed to create a healthy ecosystem. Lose one and a link in the food chain snaps.

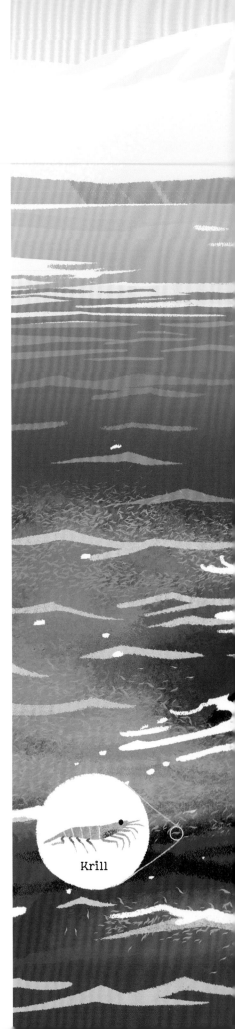

Krill

MIGRATION: THE OCEAN'S MIX MASTER

Each winter, the warm, shallow lagoons of Baja California, Mexico, fill with nearly all the world's eastern North Pacific gray whales. There, females give birth to their big babies in the spring and within a month or so leave the lagoons on their way to the Arctic, where they spend the summer months feeding in the rich food-filled waters. By fall, the population of almost 27 000 whales makes its way back to Mexico. Their round-trip journey covers more than 15 000 km (9320 mi.) and is one of the longest migrations of any mammal, on land or sea.

Many other whale species also undertake long migrations. Pacific Ocean humpback whales travel between the North Pacific and their wintering grounds in Hawaii, Mexico, Central America or Japan. And fin whales in the southern hemisphere migrate between the Antarctic and the warmer waters of Australia, New Zealand and the South Pacific islands.

Just as whales help mix the ocean by diving up and down, these twice-yearly trips help, too. Whales undertake these long swims to follow their food. Cooler waters tend to have more nutrients and food, so the whales are traveling between cooler, food-rich waters at the north or south pole, to warmer, nutrient-poor waters in the tropics and subtropics, where they mate and give birth.

As the whales swim, dive, eat, give birth, poop and generally go about living while traveling the world's oceans, they're delivering nutrients from nutrient-rich sites to those that are nutrient-poor, helping to feed plankton and fuel ocean food webs.

Humpback Whale Migration Routes

In summer, humpback whales live in the North Pacific where they feed on an abundance of small fish and plankton. In winter, they migrate to the warmer waters near Japan, Hawaii, Mexico and Central America to breed.

RUSSIA

Summer feeding area

ASIA

Alaska

CANADA

Migration route

JAPAN

Migration route

Migration route

Migration route

UNITED STATES

MEXICO

Hawaii

CENTRAL AMERICA

WHALES HELP THE PLANET

Indigenous Peoples living on the world's coastlines have always looked to the sea for food. They fish and gather seafood, and, in some cases, hunt whales. Traditionally, whale meat and oil were important sources of food and fuel, and the massive bones were often used for various structures. Some populations still continue to harvest whales for use in their communities.

But for two hundred years or so, a very different type of whale hunt developed: commercial whalers from Europe and America started to use steam-powered ships and powerful harpoons. Starting in the late 1800s, whales were killed to make products for the markets of Europe and North America. Lamps were lit and clocks were lubricated with whale oil. Whale meat was fed to pets, and umbrellas, hoop skirts and brushes were made from their baleen. Whales were seen as a resource, just like trees or oil or minerals, and were harvested for human use.

Whales were hunted hard until the end of the 1960s, when most commercial whaling finally stopped. But by then it was too late, or almost too late, for many populations to recover. An estimated three million whales had been removed from the ocean.

But while many whale populations are still endangered, others seem to be recovering. That's good news for the whales — and also good news for the world! Because scientists believe that more whales make a healthier ocean and a healthier planet.

Instead of looking at whales only as a source of oil, baleen and meat, scientists are doing the math and discovering how much whales — alive, that is — do for us and other living things. New research shows that they could even be unsung warriors in our fight against **climate change.**

THINGS ARE HEATING UP

If you've ever been in a greenhouse, you'll know it's toasty inside. The sun's rays heat up the air, and the glass in the walls and roof traps that warmth inside. Even at night, as it cools outside, the air and soil in the greenhouse stay quite warm.

In many ways, our planet and its atmosphere (the air that surrounds it) act as a giant greenhouse. As the sun's rays shine down, they warm the land and the oceans. The **gases** in the atmosphere trap in that heat, just as in a greenhouse. This keeps our planet warm and is one of the things that make life on Earth — from water lilies to whales, hummingbirds to humans — possible.

But in the last few hundred years, human activities have been adding more and more gases to our atmosphere. These gases come from factories and fires, from the cars we drive and the buildings we

heat. This extra gas traps more heat and, as a result, the planet's temperature is rising. This is called **global warming**.

During the last century, Earth's average temperature increased by about 1°C (1.8°F). That might not sound like much, but even a small rise in temperature can change the climate, resulting in droughts in some places and fiercer storms in others. Changes in climate also affect the ability of plants to grow in certain places, which disrupts food webs.

Global warming and the climate change that comes with it are the most serious issues affecting our planet. Some people, though, are working hard to make changes that help put the brakes on the rising heat. One thing that helps is to keep natural places intact and healthy — forests full of trees, rivers full of fish ... and oceans full of whales.

CARBON IS KEY

To understand how whales can affect our climate and might help us with the colossal challenge of global warming, you need to know a bit about an element called **carbon**.

All living things contain carbon. It's essential for life on Earth. And it's everywhere — in plants and animals, soil and rocks, even the air around us.

A camel, a cactus and a caterpillar may look wildly different, but they all contain carbon, the building block of life. Carbon links with other elements, such as **oxygen**, to make the sugars, proteins and fats that build our bodies.

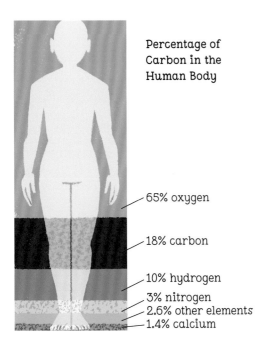

Percentage of Carbon in the Human Body

- 65% oxygen
- 18% carbon
- 10% hydrogen
- 3% nitrogen
- 2.6% other elements
- 1.4% calcium

Like you, a whale has carbon in its blood, bones, breath and in every cell in its body. And its ocean home is also where a lot of the world's carbon is hiding.

A massive carbon-filled ocean filled with massive carbon-filled whales is a big part of the story of how whales help make our planet livable.

Carbon dioxide in

Oxygen out

Oxygen in

Carbon dioxide out

CARBON ON THE MOVE

When phytoplankton make food from the sun's rays during photosynthesis, or when a blue whale eats krill, or when you eat a taco, energy is transferred through food chains. Energy is constantly cycled — or used over and over again — as plants grow and animals eat.

Carbon is constantly cycling, too. As animals eat, they pass the carbon along the food chain. The carbon in the beans and vegetables that are in your taco is passed on to you to help your body grow and function properly. And carbon is also cycled as a gas. Plants and animals move carbon in and out of the atmosphere.

As animals inhale, they take in oxygen. When they exhale, they release carbon dioxide as a waste product.

During photosynthesis, plants use the carbon dioxide from the air — along with sunlight, water and chlorophyll — to create oxygen. This reaction puts carbon into the food chain and oxygen into the atmosphere, and helps create a livable planet.

These cycles are how carbon gets from the air into plants and animals, and how it gets into our atmosphere, our soils ... and our oceans.

STORING CARBON

When plants and animals are alive, they store carbon. They pass it along if they are eaten by something, or when they breathe, poop or die. For instance, when a leaf falls or a beetle dies, carbon passes into the soil as it decays. At the same time, some carbon dioxide gas is also released into the atmosphere.

In the ocean, however, things work differently. When something dies in the ocean, it sinks and takes its carbon with it. Imagine a whale sinking to the seafloor. Scientists call this a "whale fall" — and what a bonanza it is for the animals of the deep that live far away from the phytoplankton-fueled food chains of the shallower parts of the sea. One whale can feed a lot of hungry animals. In one study, scientists counted more than sixty species feeding on a single gray whale!

And deep down in the ocean, as animals feed on the dead whale, its carbon passes along the food chain. All those carbon-filled whales feeding creatures at the bottom of the sea also help to keep the carbon out of the atmosphere.

This "export" of carbon into the deep sea is part of the reason why scientists say that having more whales in the ocean can help fight climate change.

THE CARBON CONUNDRUM

The fuels we burn to drive cars and trucks, to heat buildings and run factories, to move trains and fly planes have a surprising source: plants and animals.

That is, plants and animals that have been dead and buried for millions of years.

As phytoplankton and zooplankton and algae fell to the seafloor, and as plants such as trees and ferns died in swampy land, they became buried in the muck. Over millions of years, these dead, carbon-rich organisms piled up, and heat and pressure eventually changed that muck, or sediment, into **fossil fuels**: coal, oil (or petroleum) and natural gas. And that's what we mostly burn today to take us places, to keep us warm and to make the things we need (and many things we don't). We're digging up that trapped carbon — the remains of that buried life — and burning it, releasing the carbon as gas back into Earth's atmosphere.

And remember, too much gas in our atmosphere is why Earth's temperature is rising, causing global warming and climate change. Carbon makes our planet livable, but too much carbon in the wrong places can be a big problem.

Things are out of balance.

To help control climate change, we need to find ways to keep excess carbon out of the atmosphere.

And this is where whales come in ...

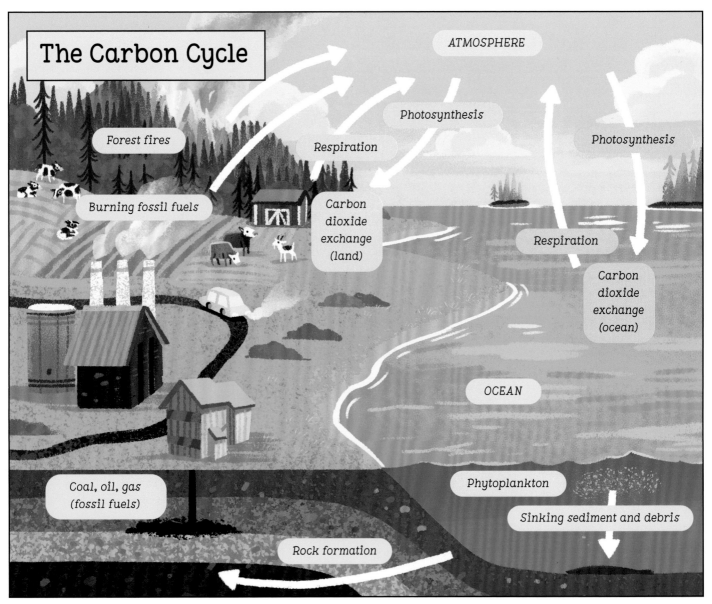

The Carbon Cycle

ATMOSPHERE

Forest fires

Photosynthesis

Respiration

Photosynthesis

Burning fossil fuels

Carbon dioxide exchange (land)

Respiration

Carbon dioxide exchange (ocean)

OCEAN

Coal, oil, gas (fossil fuels)

Phytoplankton

Sinking sediment and debris

Rock formation

WHALES TO THE RESCUE

People around the world are making changes to reduce the amount of carbon we're putting into the atmosphere. And whales are helping!

* Whales are large and live for a long time. (It's not uncommon for a whale to live eighty years or more, and a bowhead whale can live to be two hundred!) Because of their large size and long lives, whales store a lot of carbon in their bodies, and they can do this for decades, even centuries.

* As whales swim and dive and cross the world's oceans, they deposit massive amounts of nutrients into the water. This feeds phytoplankton. And as the phytoplankton use the energy of the sun during photosynthesis, they draw carbon out of the atmosphere and into the ocean.

* When whales die, they fall to the ocean floor, taking their carbon with them, where it is locked away in the deep ocean sediments.

Scientists estimate that there once were about 5 million whales in the ocean. Now there are about 1.3 million. But humans no longer kill as many whales as they once did. Instead, scientists are studying whales and learning more and more about their fascinating lives — where they travel, why some sing, how they interact with their siblings and why they sometimes leap clear out of the water, leaving their world for a moment and sailing through ours. As we learn to appreciate them, more people are working to protect whales and the habitats they depend on.

Helping whales and their ocean home helps us, too.

More whales = more poop = more phytoplankton = more carbon in the ocean = less carbon in the atmosphere.

Carbon Credits

In one study, researchers calculated that the Southern Ocean's 12 000 sperm whales remove about 200 000 t (220 000 tn.) of carbon from the atmosphere each year. That's about the same amount of carbon that 70 000 cars, each traveling about 15 000 km (9320 mi.) a year, put into the atmosphere.

HELP WHALES HELP THE PLANET

Understanding how whales help engineer ocean ecosystems shows just how complex life can be. Whales have taught us this.

And by studying how they move through the ocean, where they travel, what they eat and what happens when they die — and even calculating how much an everyday act such as pooping affects their ecosystems — we can also see how interconnected life on Earth is. Whales have a role to play, and so do we. To do all of this work for the planet, whales need a healthy ocean filled with food.

Let's try to give it to them.

GLOSSARY

alga (*plural algae*): aquatic organisms, including seaweeds and phytoplankton, that make food by photosynthesis. Unlike land plants, they do not have roots, stems, leaves or flowers.

atmosphere: the air (made up of gases) that surrounds Earth

baleen: strong, flexible strips of keratin, called plates, that attach to the upper jaws of whales and are used to filter food out of the water

carbon: a common element that is present in all living things

carbon dioxide: a gas made of carbon and oxygen

cetaceans: whales, dolphins and porpoises

chlorophyll: a green pigment found in plants and algae that traps the energy of the sun during photosynthesis

climate change: a change in climate patterns caused by an increase in carbon dioxide in the atmosphere

condense: to change from a gas into a liquid

crustaceans: animals such as crabs, shrimps and lobsters that have several pairs of legs, two pairs of antennae and a hard outer shell

echolocation: a way that certain animals navigate by making sounds and receiving the echoes that bounce off objects in front of them

ecosystem: a community of living things and how they interact with their environment

ecosystem engineer: an organism that creates, modifies or maintains a habitat or ecosystem

element: a pure substance made of one type of atom. Two examples are oxygen and carbon.

food chain: a model that shows how food energy passes from organism to organism

food web: a network of inter-connected food chains in an ecosystem

fossil fuels: coal, oil and natural gas. These are natural materials formed in Earth's crust by the compression of plant and animal matter over millions of years and are now used as fuel.

gas: a substance that spreads freely to fill the space it is in

global warming: the steady increase in the temperature of Earth's atmosphere

keratin: a hard animal protein that makes up substances such as baleen, horns, fingernails, feathers and beaks

marine snow: phytoplankton, zooplankton and other organisms that die in the ocean and then fall through the water to the seafloor

organism: an individual life-form

oxygen: a common element and a gas that is produced by the process of photosynthesis, and is used by animals as they breathe

photosynthesis: the process by which plants and algae use energy from the sun to make food

phytoplankton: floating or drifting plantlike organisms in the ocean that trap energy from the sun and convert it into food. They are the basis of marine food chains.

scavenge: to eat dead and decaying plants or animals

sediment: loose material, such as bits of rocks, soil and plant and animal remains

whale fall: a dead whale falling to the ocean floor, where it is consumed by other animals

zooplankton: the animal component of plankton. These floating or drifting organisms found in the ocean feed on other organisms.

RESOURCES

How You Can Help

Pick up litter and take part in beach cleanups. Trash on the ground often winds up in the ocean, so properly disposing of garbage helps marine wildlife.

Anything you can do to reduce excess carbon emissions is a step toward slowing climate change. Put on a sweater instead of raising the heat. Take your bike instead of riding in a car.

Plastic trash is a huge problem in the ocean. Try to avoid using single-use plastics, such as bags, cups and utensils, and recycle plastic whenever you can.

Hold a fundraiser to support organizations that help protect whales and their habitat.

Find out more about whales and share what you learn with others.

Learn More

American Cetacean Society: https://www.acsonline.org

Canadian Whale Institute: https://www.canadianwhaleinstitute.ca

Marine Education and Research Society: https://www.mersociety.org

Whale and Dolphin Conservation: https://us.whales.org

Whale Trust: https://whaletrust.org

INDEX

For Valerie Wyatt, friend and mentor, who started me on this journey
more than three decades ago — A.M.

For all the scientists, researchers and volunteers working hard for
whale conservation — K.S.

Acknowledgments

The idea of whales as ecosystem engineers is based on the work of many scientists who have spent their careers researching, publishing and sharing their knowledge. While I reviewed several research papers in the course of writing this book, I would like to specifically acknowledge the following: "Whales as Marine Ecosystem Engineers" (Joe Roman, et al.), "The Whale Pump" (Joe Roman and James McCarthy), "Southern Ocean Iron Fertilization by Baleen Whales and Antarctic Krill" (Stephen Nicol, et al.), "The Impact of Whaling on the Ocean Carbon Cycle" (Andrew Pershing, et al.) and "The Biogeochemical Role of Baleen Whales and Krill in Southern Ocean Nutrient Cycling" (Lavenia Ratnarajah, et al.). As someone who has been fortunate to write about scientific discoveries for a living — rather than having to spend long, and often tedious, hours actually making them — I am forever thankful for the dedication and effort of such researchers.

Thank you to Erich Hoyt, research fellow with Whale and Dolphin Conservation, for reviewing the manuscript and also for your book *Orca: A Whale Called Killer* that made a great and lasting impression on an 18-year-old me. Props also to Kiron Mukherjee of the Royal Ontario Museum, who helped me sort out a few details of a blue whale heart.

Thank you also to the tag team of Jennifer Stokes and Jude Isabella, who led me to this book, and to Jude again for her generosity and friendship over the years. Huzzah, huzzah, "Gillymot." And the fine team at Kids Can Press, particularly Katie Scott, was a delight to work with and good-natured about my seemingly endless tinkering.

Finally, despite close attention to detail, I've been in this game long enough to know that errors can still sometimes appear. For these, I take full responsibility.

Published in Canada and the U.S. by Kids Can Press Ltd.
25 Dockside Drive, Toronto, ON M5A 0B5

Kids Can Press is a Corus Entertainment Inc. company.

www.kidscanpress.com

The artwork in this book was rendered in Photoshop.
The text is set in Pleuf Pro.

Edited by Jennifer Stokes and Katie Scott
Designed by Marie Bartholomew

Printed and bound in Shenzhen, China, in 3/2022 by C&C Offset

CM 22 0 9 8 7 6 5 4 3 2 1

Library and Archives Canada Cataloguing in Publication

Title: Whales to the rescue : how whales help engineer the planet / written by Adrienne Mason ; illustrated by Kim Smith.
Names: Mason, Adrienne, author. | Smith, Kim, 1986- illustrator.
Description: Series statement: Ecosystem guardians | Includes index.
Identifiers: Canadiana 20210349956 | ISBN 9781525305375 (hardcover)
Subjects: LCSH: Whales — Juvenile literature. | LCSH: Whales — Ecology — Juvenile literature.
Classification: LCC QL737.C4 M385 2022 | DDC j599.5 — dc23

Kids Can Press gratefully acknowledges that the land on which our office is located is the traditional territory of many nations, including the Mississaugas of the Credit, the Anishnabeg, the Chippewa, the Haudenosaunee and the Wendat peoples, and is now home to many diverse First Nations, Inuit and Métis peoples.

We thank the Government of Ontario, through Ontario Creates; the Ontario Arts Council; the Canada Council for the Arts; and the Government of Canada for supporting our publishing activity.